They tramped along Pennsylvania's dusty roads beneath a summer sun in three long, ragged columns – 70,000 soldiers in gray and butternut, followed by artillery caissons and supply wagons. Although well-behaved for an invading army, they presented a formidable, unforgettable appearance: "Most of the men were exceedingly dirty, some ragged, some without shoes," noted eyewitnesses, "(but they were) well armed and under perfect discipline. They seemed to move like one vast machine." They were the troops of General Robert E. Lee's Army of Northern Virginia and in June of 1863 they had brought the war to the North.

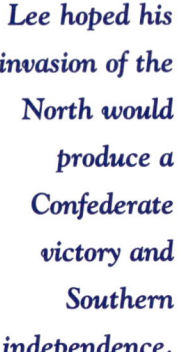

Lee hoped his invasion of the North would produce a Confederate victory and Southern independence.

Fresh from a major victory over Northern forces at the Battle of Chancellorsville, Lee's army was at the peak of strength and confidence. Although usually outnumbered, Lee's masterful maneuvering had defeated one Northern general after another. After two years of warfare and a string of serious Southern losses in the war's Western Theater, Confederate leaders believed it was time to take the fighting to Northern soil. They hoped a successful invasion would press Northerners to make peace, perhaps spur France and England to officially recognize the Confederacy, or most importantly, produce the victory that would end the war and achieve Southern independence.

Lee and his Army of Northern Virginia

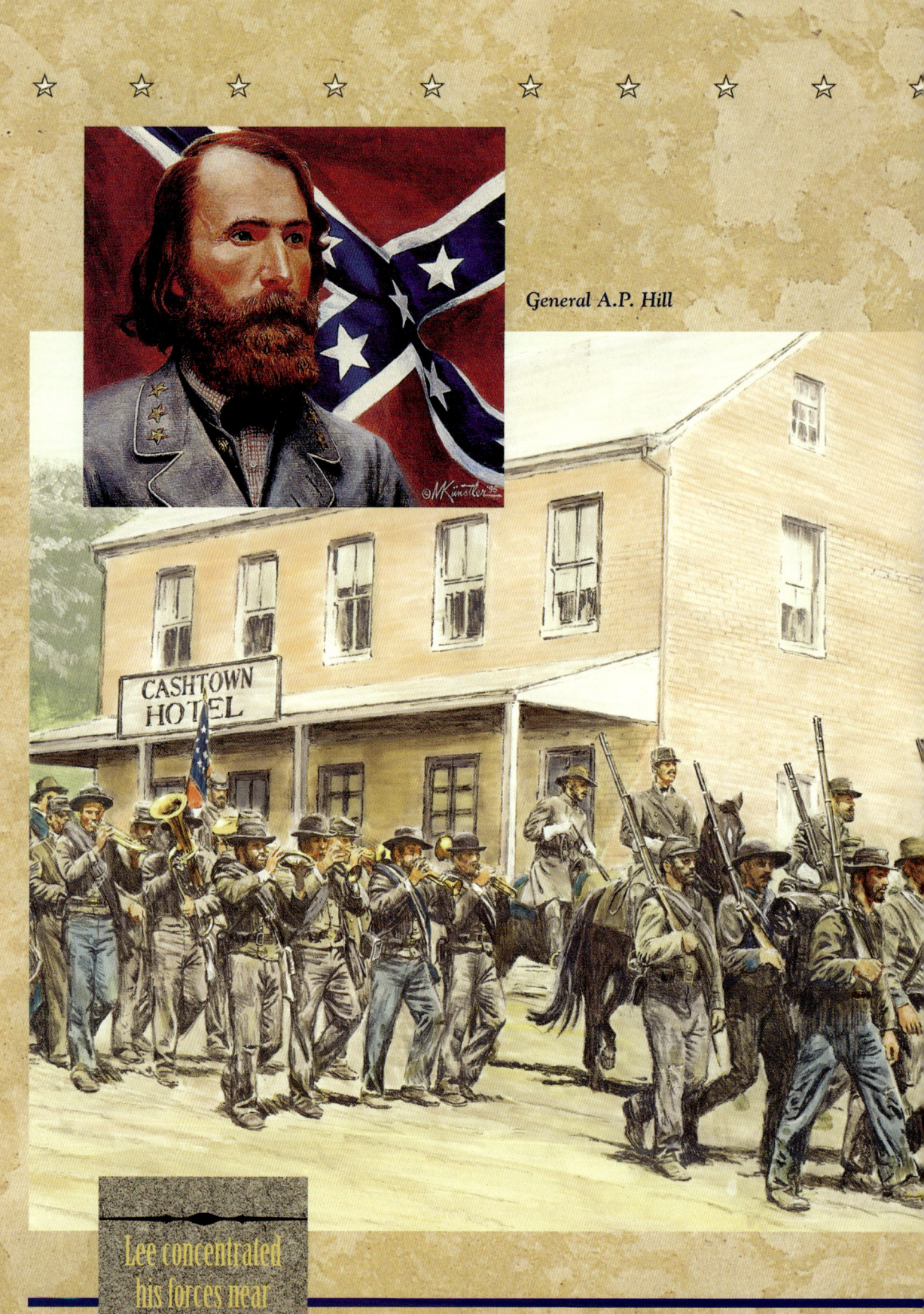

General A.P. Hill

Lee concentrated his forces near Cashtown

General George Meade was the newest commander of the Federal Army of the Potomac.

By June 30, Lee's army was spread across south–central Pennsylvania. General James Longstreet's I Corps was bivouacked near Chambersburg; the II Corps under General Richard S. Ewell was north of Gettysburg; and General A.P. Hill's III Corps was camped between Gettysburg and Chambersburg at Cashtown. President Abraham Lincoln and other Northern officials feared Lee's army would seize Harrisburg, Pennsylvania's capital, strike at Philadelphia or even manage to attack Washington, D.C. Lincoln had put a new commander, General George G. Meade, in charge of the Army of the Potomac, which had been ordered into Pennsylvania to locate and intercept the Confederate invaders. Meade was a native of Pennsylvania, which Lincoln hoped would be an advantage in stopping the Confederates. Said Lincoln: "Meade will fight well on his own dunghill."

General J.E.B. Stuart, Lee's cavalry commander, had taken his troops on a time-consuming raid that kept Lee from receiving timely intelligence.

As his army moved through the unfamiliar Pennsylvania countryside, Lee was at a disadvantage: he did not know the location of the Northern army. General J.E.B. Stuart, who was charged with reconnaissance for Lee's army, had taken his cavalry far to the east on a raid that deprived Lee of the "eyes of the army." On June 28, after learning from a spy that Meade's army was nearby, Lee hurriedly concentrated his forces near Cashtown. Two days later, a brigade of Confederate troops from Hill's Corps headed east toward the crossroads town of Gettysburg on a reconnaissance-in-force. When they spotted Northern cavalry in the distance, they withdrew to Cashtown and reported the sighting.

Buford at Gettysburg

DAY 1

★ ★ ★ ★ ★ ★ ★ ★ ★

Buford's cavalry stubbornly held their ground

Armed with rapid-firing carbines, Buford's veteran troops delayed the Confederate advance until Federal reinforcements reached Gettysburg.

Buford deployed his Federal cavalry in the path of Lee's army.

Shortly after daybreak on Wednesday, July 1, 1863, a detachment of General John Buford's Federal cavalry posted a few miles northwest of Gettysburg discovered Confederate troops marching toward them on the road from Cashtown. The troops belonged to General Henry Heth's division of Hill's Corps, and promptly attacked Buford's dismounted cavalry, igniting the Battle of Gettysburg. Although outnumbered, Buford's troops were armed with rapid-fire carbines, which helped even the odds. They made a stubborn defense, slowly falling back from ridge to ridge, stalling the Confederate advance. Finally, at about 10 a.m., General John F. Reynolds arrived with a full corps of Federal troops and another corps close behind. Reynolds deployed his troops in strong defensive positions west and north of town. When General Heth ordered an all-out assault on the Federal lines, his troops encountered Federal infantry in full force. The Confederates were initially repulsed and hundreds were captured. The Federals, however, also suffered a major loss: General Reynolds, directing the battle from horseback, was shot from the saddle and killed.

Despite their fierce resistance, Northern forces were forced to retreat on the battle's first day.

Soon afterwards, two divisions of fresh Confederate troops under General Richard S. Ewell arrived from the north, pitched into the battle and turned the Federal's right flank. The Federal line crumpled and Northern troops began streaming through Gettysburg in a disorderly retreat. A half-mile south of town on Cemetery Hill they were rallied by General Winfield S. Hancock, and were reorganized in a strong defensive position along Cemetery Ridge. Ewell received orders from Lee to take Cemetery Hill "if practicable," but chose not to attack. The battle's first day ended in a decisive Confederate victory, but by the time General George Meade arrived to take command late that night, the Federals were well-fortified on Cemetery Ridge.

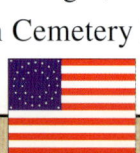

DAY 1

Lee was victorious the first day.

General Robert E. Lee

General James Longstreet urged Lee to withdraw from Gettysburg and wait for a Federal Attack.

When the battle's second day began, the Federal line was shaped like a fishhook, with the curved hook bending west from Gulp's Hill to Cemetery Ridge and the shank stretching south along Cemetery Ridge to the eye of the hook at the base of Little Round Top. Lee's army paralleled the Federal line, stretching along the Emmitsburg Road and Seminary Ridge, and bending through the edge of town and facing Culp's Hill. General James Longstreet urged Lee to take the tactical defense by withdrawing to a strong point between the Federal army and Washington, D.C. and then wait – for a Federal attack. Lee disagreed, believing the great victory he sought could be won at Gettysburg. "I am going to whip them," he told Longstreet, "or they are going to whip me."

General James Longstreet

His plans, however, were affected by unusual circumstances and his own tactical decisions. The recent death of General Thomas J. ("Stonewall") Jackson – the officer Lee called "my right arm" – denied Lee the services of his best commander. Without reconnaissance from Stuart's cavalry, Lee was unable to quickly assess the size and location of Federal forces, and his subordinate commanders were slow to execute his orders. Meade's army of 88,000 had the benefit of superior numbers and – thanks to savvy judgement by Buford and Hancock – Meade's troops also had the advantage of well-selected defensive positions. Despite repeated defeats and poor leadership in the past, the Army of the Potomac had matured into a seasoned fighting force. "You can whip them time and again," noted a Northern officer, "but the next fight they go into, they are as full of pluck as ever...."

DAY 2

Repeated assaults failed to break the Federal line

Battle of Gettysburg situation map: day one.

Battle of Gettysburg situation map: day two.

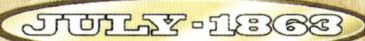

Battle of Gettysburg situation map: day three.

Lee and his staff

General John Bell Hood

General J. L Chamberlain

Federal troops rushed to defend Little Round Top.

At Gettysburg, the offensive tactics that Lee hoped would defeat the Army of the Potomac proved costly and unsuccessful after the first day. On July 2nd, advised by General Ewell that Federal positions on Gulp's Hill and Cemetery Hill were too strong to assault, Lee ordered Longstreet to attack the Federal left. Not until almost four o'clock on July 2nd did Longstreet launch the attack. By then, Meade had strengthened his line along Cemetery Ridge and on a rise of ground known as the Peach Orchard. Longstreet sent two divisions under Generals John Bell Hood and Lafayette McLaws against the Federal left, defended by troops of General Daniel E. Sickles' III Corps. Furious fighting raged through the Peach Orchard, the Wheatfield, Devil's Den and on to Little Round Top. At the peak of battle, Confederate forces appeared ready to break through the Federal line north of Little Round Top, but a courageous stand by 262 troops of the 1st Minnesota preserved the line – at a cost of 215 dead and wounded Minnesotans.

Led by Colonel Joshua L. Chamberlain, the troops of the 20th Maine repulsed a mighty Confederate assault on the battle's second day and preserved the Federal line.

The Southerners again threatened to carry the day at Little Round Top, where the extreme left flank of the Federal line was defended by the 20th Maine Infantry. Commanded by a former college professor, Colonel Joshua Lawrence Chamberlain, the regiment was under orders to hold its position "at all hazards." Repeatedly, Chamberlain and his troops repelled courageous Confederate attacks until the bloodied regiment was almost out of ammunition. Then Chamberlain ordered the unexpected: a bayonet charge. The soldiers from Maine fixed bayonets and, led by Chamberlain, met the next Southern assault with a valiant counterattack that repulsed the exhausted Confederates and saved the day for the Union. Near dark, Ewell finally launched an assault on the Federal right, but failed to take Gulp's Hill or Cemetery Hill. Despite a fierce and bloody battering, the Federal line had not broken.

Stuart joined Lee the second night.

Lee ordered Longstreet to attack the Federal center.

On July 3rd, more than 10,000 Northern and Southern horse soldiers collided in a ferocious cavalry battle.

In the early hours of July 3, General Meade sought advice from his corps commanders. "Stay and fight it out," they told him. Across the battlefield at Confederate heaquarters, Lee too had resolved to fight on. He had tried unsuccessfully to break both Federal flanks; on the third day of battle he would strike the center of his enemy's line, hoping for a breakthrough that would give the South its vitally needed victory. During the night, Stuart's cavalry had finally arrived – too late to provide Lee with desperately needed reconnaissance. Before dawn, fighting erupted at Culp's Hill, prompting a series of bloody but futile assaults by Ewell's Confederates that shredded the bark off trees and left scores of dead Southerners. Meanwhile, Lee ordered J.E.B. Stuart to take his 6,500 horse soldiers and attack the Federal rear; instead, Stuart's troops were blocked by a ferocious counterattack of 4,500 Federal cavalry three miles east of Gettysburg.

In a mile-long line, more than 13,000 Southern troops advanced.

To shatter the Federal center, Lee ordered Longstreet to direct a massive infantry assault, spearheaded by General George E. Pickett's fresh division of Virginians. Again Longstreet objected, urging Lee to withdraw and maneuver the Northern army into taking the offensive. Lee, however, was confident his army could prevail at Gettysburg. "The enemy is there," he said, pointing to Cemetery Ridge, "and I am going to strike him." At 1 p.m., as many as 170 Confederate artillery pieces opened fire, pounding the center of the Federal line with a monstrous barrage. The Northern artillery fiercely returned the fire and the battleground was smothered in smoke and dust. Although much of the Confederate barrage overshot its target, the Federal artillery fire slackened at one point, which encouraged Confederate hopes that the Northern artillery had been subdued by the barrage. The 28-year-old officer in charge of Lee's artillery, Colonel Edward Porter Alexander, sent word that his ammunition was running out. "If you are coming at all you must come immediately," he warned Longstreet.

"Up men, and to your posts!" ordered Pickett.

DAY 3

Northern troops fired from behind a stone wall.

"High Tide of the Confederacy"

Despite Southern valor and sacrifice, the Federal line heroically held.

Longstreet gave the command, and General Pickett ordered the attack: "Up men, and to your posts! Don't forget today that you are from old Virginia!" It was about three o'clock on the afternoon of Friday, July 3, 1863. From the woods on Seminary Ridge appeared more than 13,000 veteran Confederate troops. They were organized into three divisions commanded by Generals Pickett, James J. Pettigrew and Isaac R. Trimble. Across the open, sprawling Pennsylvania countryside, they advanced beneath unfurled battle flags as if on parade, moving resolutely toward a clump of trees that marked the center of the Federal line on Cemetery Ridge. It was a magnificent spectacle, which appeared "fearfully irresistible" according to a Federal observer. But it was short-lived.

"It's all my fault," Lee told the Southern survivors.

The Federal artillery opened fire with explosive shells, blasting great gaps in the Southern ranks. On they came, clambering over rail fences, crossing the Emmitsburg Road, charging up the sloping field toward the stone fence atop Cemetery Ridge. A firestorm from the Federal line devastated the ranks. On the left, troops from the 26th North Carolina, part of Pettrigrew's Division, made the farthest advance. Virginians led by General Lewis A. Armistead scaled the stone wall and momentarily pierced the Federal line, but they were beaten back and Armistead was mortally wounded. Fierce fire from the Northern defenders turned back the bloodied Confederate survivors, who streamed to the Confederate rear. There they were met by Lee, who told them, "It's all my fault."

DAY 3

Lee and Longstreet after the battle.

Lee's army retreated in the rain.

Pickett's Charge was the climax of the three-day Battle of Gettysburg – the greatest battle ever fought on the North American continent. The battle produced more than 50,000 casualties: estimated at 28,000 Confederate and 23,000 Federal. Never again would the South seem so close to winning the war: Pickett's Charge became known as the "High Tide of the Confederacy." The war would wage its bloody way for almost two more years, but the Battle of Gettysburg preserved the Union for the North and doomed the South's quest for independence. It was the turning point of the American Civil War.

In his Gettysburg Address on November 19, 1863, President Lincoln declared Gettysburg to be hollowed ground.

Mort Künstler is America's foremost painter of historical subjects. His works have been showcased in ten one-man exhibitions at New York's prestigious Hammer Galleries and at leading museums throughout the country. Künstler has been honored with the first one-man exhibition of original paintings ever shown at the Gettysburg National Military Park and the North Carolina Museum of History in Raleigh. His books include **The American Spirit** with Henry Steele Commager and two best-sellers with text by Pulitzer Prize-winning historian James McPherson: **Gettysburg** and **Images of the Civil War**. The latter book was made into a one-hour special on the Arts and Entertainment Network's **Time Machine**. Künstler's latest book is **Jackson & Lee: Legends in Gray, The Paintings of Mort Künstler**, with text by famed historian James I. Robertson, Jr. Mr. Künstler and his family live in Oyster Bay, New York.

Photo by Michael Fairchild

Historian Rod Gragg is the author of **The Civil War Quiz & Fact Book, The Illustrated Confederate Reader, Confederate Goliath: The Battle of Fort Fisher** and other books about the War Between the States.